Mark Ziaian
World Cup 2014 Full Match Reports, 73 p + Index

Copyright 2021 Intermedia Educational Co. Ltd
ISBN 978-1-896574-07-3

Published, 2021, by Transmedia Translating and Publishing
Co., a branch of Intermedia Educational Co. Ltd, 2701-2
Forest Laneway, Toronto, Ontario, M2N 5X7.
Phone:1-647-454-0220.
Email: intermediaeducational@gmail.com
Printed and distributed by Kindle Direct Publishing,
Amazon

Cover: Mark Ziaian, image attributed to freepik.com

World Cup 2014

Full Match Reports

By Mark Ziaian

About the author

Mark Ziaian is an English journalist accredited by FIFA and is also the inventor of the Ziaian football rankings system at rankfootball.com.
Mark has written mostly for Score and has reported on World Cups, the Euros, Copa America, the Asian Cup, the Africa Cup of Nations, the Olympics, Confederations Cups, the Premier League, the FA Cup, women's World Cups, youth World Cups and international friendly matches.

Table of Contents

The road to Brazil

On October 30th 2007 Brazil was elected by FIFA to host the 2014 World Cup.

Bhutan, Brunei, Guam and Mauritania did not enter the competition and South Sudan joined FIFA too late to take part in qualification. Mauritius withdrew due to lack of funding and Bahamas, who had cruised past the Turks & Caicos Islands, threw in the towel as their national stadium was under construction and they did not wish to play their home matches in another country for financial reasons. Syria were disqualified for fielding an ineligible player.in the second round matches against Tajikistan.

CONCACAF – The World Cup qualifiers kicked off on 15 June 2011 with Deon McCaulay scoring the first goal of the competition and claiming a hat-trick for Belize in their 5-2 win over Montserrat played in Trinidad & Tobago.

After the five weakest teams were eliminated, round 2 saw 6 groups of 4 teams produce El Salvador, Guyana, Panama, Canada, Guatemala and Trinidad & Tobago as group winners to join the seeded United States, Mexico, Honduras, Jamaica, Costa Rica and Cuba to form 3 groups of 4 teams with the top 2 from each group progressing to the next round to play a mini league where the top teams of U.S.A Costa Rica and Honduras qualified for the World Cup, while Mexico had to be content with an intercontinental play-off spot.

Asia – The first 2 rounds filtered out the continent's weakest teams, leaving the survivors and seeded teams to be drawn into 5 groups of 4 teams

1

with the top 2 from each group making it through to the next round where the 10 teams were drawn into 2 groups. Japan, who had finished below Uzbekistan in the previous round, became the first team after hosts Brazil to qualify for the World Cup and were followed by Iran, South Korea and Australia. Jordan and Uzbekistan, who finished third in their groups, met home and away for an intercontinental play-off place against the team finishing fifth in South America, and after drawing both matches 1-1 the Jordanians prevailed 9-8 on penalties.

Oceania – with no guaranteed representation in the World Cup finals from this section, the 11 members played for the chance to meet the fourth-best team from CONCACAF in a two-legged play-off to qualify for the World Cup in Brazil.

The 4 lowest ranked teams in the region played one another in Samoa with the hosts winning the group to join the seeded teams in the OFC Nations Cup hosted by Solomon Islands. Despite Tahiti winning the OFC Nations Cup, the 4 semi-finalist competed on equal terms to reach the intercontinental play-offs and New Zealand succeeded.

Africa – The 24 lowest ranked teams were drawn to play a home and away knockout round and the winners joined the remaining teams in the second round to play in 10 groups of 4 teams with the top teams from each group progressing the next round.

Ethiopia won group A ahead of South Africa despite having their 2-1 win in Botswana awarded 3-0 to their hosts for fielding an ineligible player and were joined in the final round by other group winners Tunisia, Ivory Coast, Ghana, Burkina Faso, Nigeria, Egypt, Algeria, Cameroon and Senegal where the teams were drawn into 5 home and away ties with the winners qualifying for the World Cup.

Algeria qualified on the away goals rule at the expense of Burkina Faso together with Ivory Coast, Nigeria and Cameroon, Ghana.

South America – With Brazil qualifying as hosts, the remaining 9 teams met in a home and away league system with the top 4 teams of Argentina, Colombia, Chile and Ecuador qualifying directly for the World Cup while Uruguay missed out on goal difference and had to face the intercontinental play-offs.

Europe – The 53 teams were drawn into 8 groups of 6 teams and a group of 5 teams with the top teams from each group qualifying for the World Cup and the 8 best runners-up (not counting games against the sixth-placed teams in their groups) entering a home and away play-off round the determine the remaining 4 qualifiers. The runners-up miss out on the play-offs were Denmark.

Belgium, Italy, Germany, Netherlands, Switzerland, Russia, Bosnia & Herzegovina, England and Spain qualified as group winners.

Play offs – In the intercontinental play-offs, Uruguay did the damage with 5 goals in Jordan and rested on their laurels at home to draw 0-0 and qualify for the finals while Mexico won home and away against New Zealand to qualify with a 9-3 aggregate.

In the European play-offs, France overturned a 2-0 loss in Ukraine with 3 goals in Paris while Christian Ronaldo scored all the Portuguese goals as they defeated Sweden 1-0 at home and 3-2 in Stockholm. Having celebrated a 3-1 victory at home, Greece held Romania to a 1-1 draw in Bucharest while Croatia retuned from a goalless draw in Iceland to book their tickets to Brazil with 2 goals in Zagreb.

Group A

Neymar points the way

Brazil 3 Croatia 1 (Sao Paulo)

Brazil came from behind to pick up 3 points in a 3-1 win with a double from Neymar against Croatia in the opening match of the 2014 World Cup.

The hosts gifted Croatia a goal in the 11th minute when Marcelo turned a low cross into his own net, but in the 29th minute Neymar rolled the ball in off the post from outside the area to level the score and in the 69th minute, when Brazil were awarded a soft penalty, Neymar forced his spot kick past Pletikosa who could only push the ball into the net.

Julio Cesar did well to block a shot from Perisic in stoppage time and moments later Oscar ran towards goal to stab the ball in from the edge of the box, ending a controversial match with a win for the hosts.

Group A

Mexico get justice

Mexico 1 Cameroon 0 (Natal)

Having had two goals disallowed, a single goal gave Mexico a winning start over Cameroon in driving rain.

Giovani dos Santos had goals harshly disallowed for offside in the 12th and 29th minute, but received a swift pass in the 61st minute and fired a low shot which Itandje did well to keep out only for Oribe Peralta to score from the rebound.

Ochoa made a spectacular save from a powerful Moukandjo header in stoppage time to ensure Mexico a deserved win.

Group B

Deadly Dutch destroy Spain

Netherlands 5 Spain 1 (Salvador)

The Netherlands ripped world champions Spain apart 5-1 after falling behind to a penalty kick.

Alonso slotted home from the spot after Spain were awarded a penalty in the 26th minute, but a minute from the interval Robin van Persie got on the end of a long ball from Blind with a mejestic diving header to steer the ball over Casillas and level the score.

In the 53rd minute Robben brought the ball down on the edge of the box, brushed off two defenders and knocked it past Casillas to put the Dutch into the lead. Van Persie volleyed the ball off the bar on the hour mark and 4 minutes later a cross from a free kick was headed down and in by Stefan de Vrij at the far post. A blunder by Cassillas in dealing with a back-pass let van Persie in for the fourth in the 72nd minute and in the 80th minute Robben darted towards goal, twisted and turned past the keeper to bang in the fifth.

Casillas made a double-save to deny the Dutch their sixth in the 87th minute and in stoppage time Torres was denied a tap-in to sum up Spain's miserable evening.

Group B

Quick firing Chile down Australia

Chile 3 Australia 1 (Cuiaba)

Two early goals in quick succession gave Chile victory over Australia.

In the 12th minute Chile showed determination to keep the ball in the box and Alexis Sanchez knocked the ball in between the keeper and the post. Two minutes later Australia looked doomed when Valdivia received the ball on the edge of the area and dispatched the ball into the roof of the net, but Australia fought back and in the 35th minute Tim Cahill rose to meet a cross and head the ball over Bravo in the Chile goal.

Bravo got down to save a volley from Bresciano in the 56th minute while 5 minutes later at the other end Vargas poked the ball past the keeper but saw Wilkinson clear off the line in the nick of time. Chile sealed their win in stoppage time when Pinilla's shot was blocked and Beausejour drove in the return crisply from outside the area.

Group C

Greeks easy for Colombia

Colombia 3 Greece 0 (Belo Horizonte)

Greece offered very little resistance as Colombia struck 3 times to start their campaign with a win.

Palbo Armero's shot took a deflection and rolled into the goal as early as the 5th minute but Colombia had to wait until the 58th minute to find the net again when a corner kick was helped on to Teofilo Gutierrez who stabbed the ball in from a yard out.

In the 63rd minute Gekas hit the underside of the bar for Greece with a diving header inside the 6-yard box and Colombia added salt to injury when James Rodriguez stroked the ball home from just inside the box in stoppage time.

Group D

Costa Rica shock Uruguay

Costa Rica 3 Uruguay 1 (Forteleza)

Group D minnows Costa Rica stunned Uruguay with a well-earned 3-1 victory.

Uruguay were awarded a penalty in the 22nd minute and Edinson Cavani struck low and hard from the spot to give the South Americans the lead. Forlan's deflected shot just before the break was brilliantly tipped over the bar by Navas, but in the 54th minute Joel Campbell chested a cross in the box and whacked in the equaliser. Only 3 minutes later a free kick was floated into the box for Oscar Duarte to stoop and head in across goal and in the 84th minute a clever pass from Campbell on the right found substitute Marcos Urena who rolled the ball past the keeper into the far corner.

Maxi Pereira was shown a straight red for Uruguay in stoppage time when he took a swipe at Campbell who was protecting the ball near the corner flag.

Group D

England tumble in the jungle

Italy 2 England 1 (Manaus)

Mario Balotelli scored the winner as Italy got the better of England at the Arena Amazonia in Manaus.

In the 35th minute a clever dummy from Pirlo after a well-worked corner set up Claudio Marchisio who found the corner of the net with a daisy-cutter past the diving Hart, but 2 minutes later Daniel Sturridge got on the end of a Rooney cross to knock in the equaliser.

In first half stoppage time Balotelli chipped Hart but saw his effort headed off the line by Jagielka and moments later Candreva's angled shot struck the base of the England post. In the 58th minute Candreva curled in a cross for Balotelli to head home at the far post.

Sirigu was kept busy in the Italy goal and Pirlo came close when his swerving free kick bounced off the bar in stoppage time.

Group C

Elephants hit back

Ivory Coast 2 Japan 1 (Recife)

Two goals in as many minutes for Ivory Coast turned the table on Japan.

Keisuke Honda gave Japan the lead in the 16th minute when he slammed a left-footer into the roof of the net from just inside the area, but in the 64th minute Wilfried Bony flung himself to meet a cross from Aurier and beat Kawashima with a glancing header and 2 minutes later Gervinho got on the end of another cross from Aurier to head low between the keeper and the post.

Group E

Late Swiss delight

Switzerland 2 Ecuador 1 (Brasilia)

Switzerland grabbed a last gasp winner in their first group-match over Ecuador.

Ayovi delivered a free kick from the left flank onto the head of Enner Valencia who headed down and into the net from inside the 6-yard box in the 22nd minute, but the Swiss were level 2 minutes after the break when substitute Amir Mehmedi headed in a corner-kick from a similar position.

Deep into stoppage time, after foiling an Ecuador attack, Switzerland broke through with substitute Haris Seferovic dispatching a low delivery into the roof of the net from in front of goal with his first touch of the game to bank all 3 points.

Group E

France punish physical Honduras

France 3 Honduras 0 (Porto Alegre)

Karim Benzema scored twice as France asserted their superiority over Honduras.

Wilson Palacios who had been booked for an earlier altercation with Pogba was dismissed after giving away a penalty, which Bezema converted with aplomb 2 minutes before the break.

Three minutes after reconvening, goal line technology was used for the first time in a World Cup match when Benzema met the ball on the run and knocked it from the edge of the 6-yard box onto the far post and over the line via the scrambling goalkeeper Valladares at the near post for an own-goal. In the 72nd minute Debuchy's thunderous shot was deflected into the path of Benzema who slammed the ball in from a tight angle for the third.

Group F

Bosnia rue early gift

Argentina 2 Bosnia & Herzegovina 1
(Rio de Janeiro)

Lionel Messi got on the scoresheet at the Maracana as Argentina edged debutants Bosnia and Herzegovina.

A free kick crossed into the box by Messi on the left went in off Sead Kolasinac for an own goal after only 3 minutes. Argentina did very little to excite the vast crowd at the Maracana until the 65th minute when Messi burst into action and curled the ball in off the base of the post from just outside the area.

Bosnia pulled a goal back 5 minutes from time when Lulic found Vedad Ibisevic who slid the ball in between the keeper's legs.

Group G

Müller hat-trick humbles Ten-man Portugal

Germany 4 Portugal 0 (Salvador)

Thomas Müller claimed the first hat-trick of the World Cup as Germany put ten-man Portugal to the sword.

Müller found the bottom left corner from the penalty spot in the 12th minute and Mats Hummel made it 2 with a thumping header from a corner kick in the 32nd minute, but Portugal's task got considerably harder 5 minutes later when Pepe was sent off for violent conduct, and on the stroke of half time a cross fell to Müller who knocked in the third.

In the 78th minute Patricio got a hand to Schuerrle' low delivery across goal and Müller was on hand to complete his hat-trick with a tap in. Cristiano Ronaldo showed what could have been, with a scorcher of a free kick in stoppage time, which Neuer did well to save.

Group F

Chanceless

Iran 0 Nigeria 0 (Curitiba)

Iran and Nigeria played out a goalless match in Curitiba with hardly any chances created by either team.

Enyeama in the Nigeria goal kept out a close-range header from Ghoochannejad in the 33rd minute. The first draw of the tournament leaves both sides with very little realistic chance of progressing to the next round.

Group G

US kick off with victory

USA 2 Ghana 1 (Natal)

Ghana came back from an early setback only to see a late American winner.

The Americans got off to a flying start when Clint Dempsey got into the box from the left, strolled past two defenders and scored in off the far post after only 31 seconds from the kick off. In the 21st minute Jozy Altidore was carried off clutching his hamstring and likely to miss the rest of the tournament.

Ghana equalised in the 82nd minute when Andre Ayew received the ball from a Gyan back heel and beat Howard at the near post with the outside of his left foot, but 4 minutes later John Brooks met a corner kick to head in the winner.

Group H

Subs save Belgium

Belgium 2 Algeria 1 (Belo Horizonte)

Belgium came from a losing position to defeat Algeria with 2 goals in the last 20 minutes.

Algeria took the lead in the 23rd minute when Sofiane Feghouli sent Courtois the wrong way from the spot. Origi came close for Belgium in the 66th minute when he was through on goal, but keeper Mbolhi stuck out a leg to block his shot.

Minutes after coming on, Marouane Fellaini flicked his header in off the bar and 10 minutes later, in the 80th minute Hazard ran from the halfway line, fed the ball into the box to Dries Mertens who smacked it high into the net for the winner.

Group A

Keeper keeps Brazil out

Brazi 0 Mexico 0 (Fortaleza)

Guillermo Ochoa proved unbeatable as Mexico held hosts Brazil to a goalless draw.

Ochoa flew to his right to claw out a header form Neymar in the 26th minute. The Mexican keeper got his body behind a Neymar shot at his near post in the 69th minute and saved point blank from a Silva header 4 minutes from time.

Julius Cesar was far less busy at the other end, but had to get down to fist away a Jimenez shot in stoppage time.

Group H

Russia hit back after howler

Russia 1 South Korea 1 (Cuiba)

South Korea and Russia shared the points in a match that will be remembered for a goalkeeping howler.

In the 68th minute Lee Keun Ho picked the ball up in the centre circle and advanced towards goal before unleashing a shot straight at Akinfeev who palmed it over the line and into his net, but 6 minutes later South Korea failed to clear after the keeper had got down to save Dzagoev's angled shot and Alexander Kerzhakov turned in the equaliser just 2 minutes after coming on.

Group B

Aussies make Dutch sweat

Netherlands 3 Australia 2 (Porto Alegre)

The Netherlands were given a scare before eventually getting past Australia.

In the 20th minute Arjen Robben went on one of his runs and slotted the ball past Mat Ryan into the far corner, but a minute later McGowan sent a high ball into the box for Tim Cahill to smash in off the crossbar with a sumptuous left-footed volley.

Australia went ahead when they were awarded a controversial penalty for handball in the 53rd minute and Mike Jedinak sent Cillessen the wrong way with a firm shot into the bottom corner of the net, but 5 minutes later Robin van Persie received the ball in the box, turned and fired high into the net.

In the 68th minute Memphis Depay's swerving shot from distance skimmed off the turf in front of the keeper and found the corner of the net for the Dutch winner.

Group B

Chile end Spanish reign

Chile 2 Spain 0 (Rio de Jeneiro)

Reigning world champions Spain became the first team to be knocked out of this year's World Cup after losing 2-0 to Chile.

In the 20th minute Aranguiz received the ball in the box and passed it to Vargas who kept his cool and knocked it in while off balanced. Two min before the break Casillas returned Alexis Sanchez's catchable free kick with a weak punch only 15 yards out to the feet of Aranguiz who toe-poked the ball past the hapless keeper.

Basquets missed a chance in front of goal for Spain in the 52nd minute and in the 68th minute Chile's Isla missed an open goal after stretching to connect with Mena's shot across goal. Iniesta curled the ball towards the top corner in the 84th minute, but Bravo acrobatically tipped the ball away to deny Spain a consolation goal.

Group A

Cameroon dumped out

Croatia 4 Cameroon 0 (Manaus)

Mario Mandzukic scored twice as Croatia put 4 past 10-man Cameroon to keep their hopes alive.

In the 11th minute a ball into the area fell to Perisic who passed it to Olic on the 6-yard line to knock into the back of the net. Cameroon were reduced to 10 men in the 40th minute when Alex Song saw red for an off-the-ball incident and 3 minutes after the break found themselves further behind when a poor clearance from Itandje found Perisic who darted into the box and beat him at the near post.

Mandzukic missed the target when through on goal in the 50th minute but headed in unchallenged from a corner kick in the 61st minute. In the 74th minute Eduardo curled a low shot that the keeper could only parry into the path of Mandzukic who tucked in his second and Croatia's fourth.

Group C

Colombia on course

Colombia 2 Ivory Coast 1 (Brasilia)

A 2-1 win over Ivory Coast all but secured passage to the next round for Colombia.

After a goalless first half, Cuardado brushed the crossbar from a tight angle in the 59th minute and 5 minutes later Colombia were ahead when James Rodriguez met a corner with a thumping header.

In the 70th minute Ivory Coast were dispossessed in the middle of the field and Colombia broke through in a swift attack culminating in Juan Quintero slotting the ball past the keeper to double their lead. Three minutes later Gervinho skipped past 3 Colombians from the left and fired in to give the African side hope.

Thursday June 19th

Group D

Suares double shatters England dreams

Uruguay 2 England 1 (Sao Paulo)

Two goals from Luis Suarz took England's destiny out of their own hands.

Rooney headed the ball against the angle of the woodwork at the far post from a Gerrard in swinging free kick in the 31st minute, but in the 39th minute Cavani found Suarez who headed past Hart to give Uruguay the lead.

In the 75th minute Johnson got into the box and sent the ball into the 6-yard area for Rooney to knock past Muslera in the Uruguay goal, but with 6 minutes remaining a long ball from Muslera skimmed of the head of Gerrard and reached Suarez who smacked it past Hart from a tight angle to give Uruguay the win.

Group C

Ten Greeks hold Japan

Japan 0 Greece 0 (Natal)

Greece and Japan shared the points to send Croatia through to the next round.

Greek captain Katsouranis was dismissed for a second yellow in the 38th minute, but Japan failed to capitalise on their numerical advantage. Uchida's ball across goal in the 68th minute found Okubo who skied it at the back post wasting Japan's best chance of the night.

Group D

Italian loss sends England home

Costa Rica 1 Italy 0 (Recife)

Costa Rica celebrated a historic win over Italy to top the group of death and send England crashing out of World Cup.

  Balotelli lifted the ball over the Costa Rica keeper in the 31st minute with no end result and struck a powerful volley at the keeper 2 minutes later, but on the stroke of half time Bryan Ruiz ran onto a cross at the far post and headed it back off the underside of the crossbar and over the line. The Italians failed to create any real chances in the second half and England's exit was confirmed.

Group E

Rampant French crush Swiss

France 5 Switzerland 2 (Salvador)

France put on a five star performance to sweep Switzerland aside.

Olivier Giroud rose to meet a corner kick and send a firm header into the top corner in the 17th minute and seconds after the restart Benzema was gifted the ball and passed it to Blaise Matuidi who beat the keeper at his near post.

France were awarded a penalty in the 31st minute but Benaglio blocked Benzema's shot and Valbuena could only knock the rebound onto the crossbar. Five minutes from the break, France hit the Swiss on a counter-attack as Giroud sprinted onto a pass down the left and fed Valbuena in the 6-yard area to make it three.

In the 67th minute Pogba chipped the ball into the box for Benzema to hook in between the keeper's legs and 5 minutes later Moussa Sissoko swept Benzema's pass into the far corner for the fifth.

The Swiss hit back with a long-distance daisy cutter from a free kick into the corner of the net in the 81st minute and in the 87th minute Inler lifted the ball over the defence for Granit Xhaka to volley past Lloris and salvage some pride.

Group E

Valencia hit Honduras with double

Ecuador 2 Honduras 1 (Curitiba)

Enner Valencia scored twice as Ecuador came from behind to beat Honduras.

The Hondurans took the lead in the 31st minute when a long clearance fell to Carlos Costly who hammered home from the 18-yard line, but 3 minutes later a shot from Paredes into the box took a deflection and was squeezed in by Valencia at the far post.

A Costly header just before the halftime whistle hit the post but the follow up was disallowed for off-side.

Ecuador got their winner in the 65th minute when Ayovi whipped in a free kick for Valencia to head in off the base of the post.

Group F

Messi magic denies Iran draw

Argentina 1 Iran 0 (Belo Horizonte)

Lionel Messsi broke Iranian hearts with a stoppage-time winner.

A well-organised Iranian side limited Argentina's chances and began to create their own after the break. Having a penalty shout turned down in the 55th minute, Iran came closest in the 67th minute when Dejagah's header was tipped over the bar, but in time-added-on Messi received the ball outside the box, took a step to the left and curled it past the diving Haghighi into the top corner to win the match and send Argentina to the next round.

Group G

Germans fight back for Ghana parity

Germany 2 Ghana 2 (Fortaleza)

Miroslav Klose came on to score with his first touch and deny Ghana victory over Germany.

The match came to life in the second half when Müller delivered the ball between two defenders in the 51st minute and Mario Götze headed the ball in off his own knee, and 3 minutes later Andre Ayew got up high to head a cross in beyond Neuer.

In the 63rd minute, Muntari slipped the ball through to Asamoah Gyan who advanced into the box and slammed it in across goal, but in the 71st minute, just moments after coming on, Klose stuck out a foot to see Höwedes' header over the line and earn Germany a point.

Group F

Nigeria send Bosnia home

Nigeria 1 Bosnia & Herzegovina 0 (Cuiaba)

Bosnia & Herzegovina were eliminated after losing their second match in a row.

The Bosnians, who had a Dzeko goal wrongly disallowed for offside in the 22nd minute, fell behind to Nigeria in the 29th minute when Emenike ran into the box and pulled the ball back for Peter Odemwingie to knock in between the keeper and the near post.

Bosnia came close to getting a lifeline with almost the last kick of the match when Dzeko turned in the box but saw his weak shot hit the keeper and come off the post.

Group H

Late rally sends Belgium through

Belgium 1 Russia 0 (Rio de Jeneiro)

Belgium booked their place in the next round with a late goal against Russia.

Kikorin failed to hit the target with a free header just before the break and the match seemed poised to end in a dull goalless draw until Belgium stepped up a gear. Mirallas hit the base of the post from a free kick in the 84th minute and with 2 minutes remaining, Hazard got to the byline and pulled the ball back for Divock Origi to fire into the roof of the net and send Belgium through.

Group H

Desert Warriors blow Korea away

Algeria 4 South Korea 2 (Porto Alegre)

Algeria kept their hopes alive with a victory over South Korea thanks to an explosive 10 minutes in the first half.

In the 26th minute Islam Slimani got onto a long ball between 2 Koreans and dinked the ball past Jung Sung Ryong, and only 2 minutes later Rafik Halliche beat the keeper to the ball from a corner kick to double the lead with a thumping header.

In the 37th minute Algeria made it 3 when a Korean defender headed down a long ball to Slimani who teed it up for Abdelmoumen Djabou to side-foot into the corner of the net. South Korea pulled a goal back 5 minutes after the break when a long ball into the box came off the back of Son Heung Min who turned and fired in between the legs of the keeper.

Ki Sung Yueng unleased a bullet from 35 yards forcing Mbolhi into a magnificent save in the 60th minute and 2 minutes later Yacine Brahimi exchanged a one-two with Feghouli and slid the ball past the keeper to restore Algeria's 3-goal lead. South Korea reduced the deficit in the 72nd minute when after a header was won in the box, the ball was tackled as far as Lee Keunho who fired it across the 6-yard area for Koo Ja Cheol to turn in.

Group G

Portugal back from the dead

Portugal 2 USA 2 (Manaus)

A last gasp equaliser against the USA rescued Portugal from elimination.

The Portuguese took a 5th minute lead when a clearance was sliced into the path of Nani who coolly rifled the ball into the roof of the net from the 6-yard line. Just before the break Nani smacked the post from outside the area and Howard made a brilliant recovery save from Eder's follow up.

In the 55th minute, Johnson got to the byline and cut the ball back to Bradley whose effort from 6 yards out was heroically cleared off the line by Costa, but the Americans levelled the score in the 64th minute when Jermaine Jones smashed a stunning shot into the corner of the net.

With 9 minutes left when a cross from the right was not cleared, the ball fell to Zusi who sent it into the 6-yard area for Clint Dempsey to chest home. Seconds away from the final whistle, with Portugal facing elimination, Ronaldo put in a delicious cross for Silvestre Varela to score with a diving header and keep Portugal's hopes in the competition alive.

Group B

Dutch earn top spot

Netherlands 2 Chile 0 (Sao Paulo)

Needing only a draw to top their group, the Netherlands put 2 past Chile for good measure.

Both teams contained each other well until the 76th minute when Depay weaved his way into position and stung the palm of Bravo. The ensuing corner was played out and crossed onto the head of the unmarked Leroy Fer who leapt high and powered the ball into the corner of the net moments after coming off the bench. The Dutch wrapped things up in stoppage time when Robben chased a long ball down the left and sent it across goal for Memphis Depay to knock in.

Group B

Spain bow out in style

Spain 3 Australia 0 (Curitiba)

In the bottom-of-the-table meeting, Spain eased past Australia to go out with a win.

In the 36th minute Juan Fran passed the ball from the byline to the 6-yard line for David Villa to score with a confident sideheel on the day he hung up his international boots. Iniesta slipped the ball through to Fernando Torres who rolled it past Ryan in the 69th minute and in the 82nd minute Juan Mata brought a cross down in front of goal and coolly nutmegged the keeper for the third.

Group A

Mexico march on

Mexico 3 Croatia 1 (Recife)

Croatia fell apart as Mexico hit 3 in 10 minutes to progress from their group.

Herrera smacked the angle of the crossbar from 25 yards in the 16th minute and in the 65th minute Corluka headed off his line after Pletikosa failed to deal with an in-swinging corner, but in the 72nd minute Mexico broke the deadlock when Rafael Marquez headed a corner down past Pletikosa. Three minutes later Peralta laid the ball on for Andres Guardado to sidefoot high into the net.

Croatia came close in the 78th minute when Rebic slalomed into the box and sidefooted past the keeper only for Moreno to clear off the line, but 4 minutes later they were further behind when a corner kick was flicked on for Javier Hernandez to head in at the far post.

Rakitic backheeled the ball for Perisic to go on and slot past the keeper into the far corner in the 87th minute, but 2 minutes later Croatia were reduced to 10 men when Rebic was shown red for a dangerous tackle. Bravo denied Croatia a consolation goal in stoppage time when he saved a spectacular close-range Perisic volley.

Group A

Neymar keeps Brazil on top

Brazil 4 Cameroon 1 (Brasilia)

Two goals from Neymar put Brazil on their way to a 4-1 win over Cameroon to top their group.

The hosts took the lead in the 17th minute when Cameroon were dispossessed and the ball was sent into the box for Neymar to open up his right foot and guide it into the far corner.

In the 20th minute Neymar's volley was palmed away and 6 minutes later Cameroon were level when Nyom's persistence on the left enabled him to put in a dangerous low cross for a Joel Matip tap in.

Brazil took the lead again in the 34th minute when Neymar cut inside to his right and sent the keeper the wrong way, and added to their tally after the break when Fred headed into an empty net from a David Luis cross in the 49th minute.

Brazil got their fourth in the 84th minute when Cameroon lost possession and after some quick interchange Fernandinho poked the ball past the keeper into the corner of the net.

Group D

Young England off target

England 0 Costa Rica 0 (Belo Horizonte)

Costa Rica finished top of the group with a goalless draw against a talented young England side representing the future of English football.

Foster tipped a 23rd minute Borges free kick over the bar, but it was England who dominated the match with Sturridge having several attempts without testing Navas in the Costa Rica goal.

Group D

Uruguay edge Italy out

Uruguay 1 Italy 0 (Natal)

Ten-man Italy failed to hold onto the draw they needed and were knocked out at the group stage.

Claudio Marchisio was shown a straight red for a high tackle a minute before the hour mark. Buffon did well to get down and save from Suarez in the 66th minute as he ran into the box and screwed the ball with the outside of his foot.

In the 79th minute Suarez was accused of biting an opponent, but the referee took no action and 2 minutes later the ball flew past Buffon off the back of Diego Godin to add salt to injury and knock Italy out of the World Cup.

Group C

Colombia put Japan to the sword

Colombia 4 Japan 1 (Cuiaba)

Jackson Martinez scored twice as Colombia thumped Japan 4-1 to complete their group matches with 3 wins.

The Japanese, who needed a win to progress, set off with determination but in a rare Colombian attack in the 16th minute gave away a penalty and Juan Cuadrado slammed the ball down the middle with the keeper diving to his right. Just as the referee was about to blow his whistle for half time, Honda delivered the ball to Shinji Okazaki who scored with a stooping header while facing away from goal.

Ten minutes after the break, Rodriguez received the ball and knocked it on to Martinez who swept it into the opposite corner. Martinez scored another in the 82nd minute when he ran onto a pass into the box, pulled the ball back rendering his marker ineffective, before curling it into the far corner. Colombia made it 4 in the last minute of the match when Martinez sent the ball through to James Rodriguez who twisted and turned past a defender before dinking it past the keeper.

Tuesday June 24th

Group C

Greeks make history

Greece 2 Ivory Coast 1 (Fortaleza)

Greece scored a penalty with the last kick of the match to knock Ivory Coast out and reach the next round for the first time ever.

In the 33rd minute Greece counter attacked after clearing an Ivory Coast corner and Cholevas rattled the bar from just outside the box, but 3 minutes before half time Ivory Coast gave the ball away and, after a one-two with Samaras, Andreas Samaris fired in over the already committed Barry.

In the 68th minute Karagounis hit the crossbar from 35 yards but 6 minutes later the ball was slotted through to Gervinho who teed up Wilfred Bony for the equaliser that would have been enough to take the Elephants through.

Torosidis hit the post with a low cross in the 80th minute, but deep into stoppage time Greece were awarded a penalty and Georgios Samaras converted confidently with the last kick of the match.

Group F

Bosnia out with win

Bosnia & Herzegovina 3 Iran 1 (Salvador)

Iran failed to get the win they needed and were knocked out 3-1 by Bosnia & Herzegovina.

Edin Dzeko struck in the 23rd minute when his accurate low shot from outside the area brushed the post as it went in. Iran went on the attack immediately after that and within a minute Shojaei hit the underside of the bar, but Bosnia doubled their lead inn the 59th minute when Iran gave the ball away and Miralem Pjanic received a pass in the box to sidefoot past Haghighi.

Iran pulled a goal back in the 82nd minute when Nekounam knocked the ball across the face of goal for Reza Ghoochannejad to score, but a minute later Avdija Vrsajevic ran into the box from the right and fired across goal in off the post to extinguish Iran's hopes

Group F

Nigeria celebrate loss

Argentina 3 Nigeria 2 (Porto Alegre)

Two goals from Messi helped Argentina to a narrow win over Nigeria who also made it to the next round thanks to Iran's failure to beat Bosnia & Herzegovina.

Argentina took a 3rd minute lead when di Maria's angled shot from inside the box ricocheted off the keeper and the post falling to Lionel Messi who smashed it into the roof of the net, but a minute later Ahmed Musa cut inside the box from the left and let fly past the diving Romero to level the score.

In the 44th minute Enyeama palmed a Messi free kick out of the top corner, but a minute into stoppage time he was not to be denied and Argentina had the lead. Two minutes after the break Musa ran into the box and drilled past Romero having sent him the wrong way, but 3 minutes later di Maria stung the palms of the keeper and the ensuing corner kick went in off the knee of Marcos Rojo for the winner.

Wednesday June 25th

Group E

Shaqiri hat-trick sends Swiss through

Switzerland 3 Honduras 0 (Manaus)

Xherdan Saqiri scored all 3 goals as Switzerland eased past Honduras into the next round.

The Swiss showed intent from the start and in the 3rd minute the Honduras keeper had to block an effort from Shaqiri who got on the end of a Drmic ball fired from the left into the 6-yard box, but 3 minutes later Shaqiri Smashed a stunner into the top corner off the bar.

In the 31st minute Shaqiri received the ball from Drmic and ran into the box to dispatch it past Valladares in the Honduras goal. Shaqiri completed his hat-trick in the 71st minute when Drmic skilfully got into the box from the left and touched the ball on for him to drill past the keeper.

Wednesday June 25ᵗʰ

Group E

French blanks not enough

France 0 Ecuador 0 (Rio de Janeiro)

Ten-man Ecuador held France at bay but failed to achieve the win they needed to go through.

Two minutes after the break, Griezmann got a foot to a cross from Sagna but Domínguez touched it onto the post. Ecuador's task got harder a minute later when their captain Antonio Valencia was sent off for showing his studs.

In the 53rd minute Ecuador broke through, but Noboa ended up slicing his shot wide. In the 72nd minute Pogba headed wide of the far post from close range. Lloris beat away Ibarra's angled shot in the 82nd minute while at the other end Domínguez had to be alert and pushed away Remi's curling shot 3 minutes from time.

Group G

Damage done

Portugal 2 Ghana 1 (Brasilia)

A 2-1 win over Ghana was not enough as Portugal crashed out of the World Cup on goal difference having suffered a 4-0 drubbing at the hands of the Germans in their first match.

Ronaldo's cross hit the bar in the 5th minute and his 19th minute point-blank header was saved by the keeper while at the other end a minute later Gyan was through only to be denied by the legs of the Portuguese keeper, but the deadlock was broken in the 30th minute when John Boye sliced a cross in off the bar and post for an own goal.

Portugal equalised in the 57th minute when Asamoah curled a beautiful ball with the outside of his left foot for Asamoah Gyan to nod in at the far post, but with 10 minutes of the match left Dauda flapped a high defensive header into the path of Ronaldo who lashed in the winner with his left foot into the bottom corner.

Group G

Americans get result

Germany 1 USA 0 (Recife)

Team USA made it to the next round on goal difference after losing only 1-0 to Germany.

The Germans dominated the match but only managed one goal when Howard got down and fisted a Mertesacker header away as far as Thomas Müllcr who curled it into the bottom right corner in the 55th minute.

A draw would have eliminated the other 2 teams regardless of their result, but America showed very little ambition to threaten the German goal.

Group H

Algeria knock Russia out

Algeria 1 Russia 1 (Curitiba)

Islam Slimani scored to earn a point and take Algeria through to the next round ahead of Russia.

The Russians took the lead in the 6th minute when Alexander Kokorin rose unchallenged to head in from a Shatov cross, but in the 60th minute a free kick was crossed beyond the Russian keeper for Slimani to head in and put Algeria on course to meet Germany in the next round.

Group H

Industrious Koreans go home

Belgium 1 South Korea 0 (Sao Paulo)

Belgium made it 3 wins out of 3 with a 1-0 win over South Korea.

In the 25th minute the ball fell to Mertens who cleared the bar from 7 yards out and 5 minutes later at the other end Coutois got down to his right to keep out a shot from Ki Sung Yeung. Just before the break, Steven Defour was shown a straight red for a 2-footed challenge.

A cross from Son bounced off the bar in the 59th minute. The Koreans failed to find a way through and were punished in the 77th minute when Sung got down to parry a shot from Origi and Jan Vertonghen buried the follow up.

Group Tables

and

Knockout Stage

Group A

Pos	Team	Pld	W	D	L	GF	GA	GD	Pts
1	Brazil	3	2	1	0	7	2	5	7
2	Mexico	3	2	1	0	4	1	3	7
3	Croatia	3	1	0	2	6	6	0	3
4	Cameroon	3	0	0	3	1	9	−8	0

Group B

Pos	Team	Pld	W	D	L	GF	GA	GD	Pts
1	Netherlands	3	3	0	0	10	3	7	9
2	Chile	3	2	0	1	5	3	2	6
3	Spain	3	1	0	2	4	7	−3	3
4	Australia	3	0	0	3	3	9	−6	0

Group C

Pos	Team	Pld	W	D	L	GF	GA	GD	Pts
1	Colombia	3	3	0	0	9	2	7	9
2	Greece	3	1	1	1	2	4	−2	4
3	Ivory Coast	3	1	0	2	4	5	−1	3
4	Japan	3	0	1	2	2	6	−4	1

Group D

Pos	Team	Pld	W	D	L	GF	GA	GD	Pts
1	Costa Rica	3	2	1	0	4	1	3	7
2	Uruguay	3	2	0	1	4	4	0	6
3	Italy	3	1	0	2	2	3	−1	3
4	England	3	0	1	2	2	4	−2	1

Group E

Pos	Team	Pld	W	D	L	GF	GA	GD	Pts
1	France	3	2	1	0	8	2	6	7
2	Switzerland	3	2	0	1	7	6	1	6
3	Ecuador	3	1	1	1	3	3	0	4
4	Honduras	3	0	0	3	1	8	−7	0

Group F

Pos	Team	Pld	W	D	L	GF	GA	GD	Pts
1	Argentina	3	3	0	0	6	3	3	9
2	Nigeria	3	1	1	1	3	3	0	4
3	Bosnia & Herzegovina	3	1	0	2	4	4	0	3
4	Iran	3	0	1	2	1	4	−3	1

Group G

Pos	Team	Pld	W	D	L	GF	GA	GD	Pts
1	Germany	3	2	1	0	7	2	5	7
2	United States	3	1	1	1	4	4	0	4
3	Portugal	3	1	1	1	4	7	−3	4
4	Ghana	3	0	1	2	4	6	−2	1

Group H

Pos	Team	Pld	W	D	L	GF	GA	GD	Pts
1	Belgium	3	3	0	0	4	1	3	9
2	Algeria	3	1	1	1	6	5	1	4
3	Russia	3	0	2	1	2	3	−1	2
4	South Korea	3	0	1	2	3	6	−3	1

Round of 16

Brazil pip Chile at the post

Brazil 1 Chile 1 (Belo Horizonte)
Brazil win on penalties

An exciting Chilean side took hosts Brazil to a penalty shootout but came up short.

Brazil scored off the knee of David Luis when a corner was headed on to him in the 18th minute, but Chile levelled the score in the 32nd minute when Vargas stole the ball from a Brazilian throw-in and passed it to Alexis Sanchez who rolled it into the far corner.

Bravo turned away a dipping shot from Alves in the 42nd minute and in the 55th minute Hulk had the ball in the back of the net but was adjudged to have used his upper arm to control it. In the 64th minute, after some quick passes from Chile, Cesar got down brilliantly to make a vital reflex save from Aranguiz and in the last minute of extra time Pinilla smashed the bar from the 18-yard line almost putting the hosts out of the competition.

In the penalty shootout David Luis sent the keeper the wrong way and Cesar saved from Pinilla, Willian rolled his shot wide and Cesar guessed right to save from Sanchez, Bravo couldn't keep Marcelo's shot out and Aranguiz slammed the ball into the top corner, Bravo saved with his knees from Hulk while Diaz levelled the proceedings with a shot down the middle.

Neymar's hesitant run sent the keeper the wrong way and with Jara hitting the inside of the post Chile were out and Brazil through to the next round.

Round of 16

Uruguay bite the dust

Colombia 2 Uruguay 0 (Rio de Janeiro)

James Rodriguez hit a double to send a toothless Uruguay home.

Rodriguez chested the ball with his back to goal and volleyed magnificently in off the bar from outside the box in the 28th minute and in the 50th minute, after some excellent teamwork, Cuadrado headed a cross back for Rodriguez to knock in from 6 yards.

Ospina made saves from distant shots, but without Suarez, who was suspended for a biting incident in the previous match, Uruguay never looked like scoring 2 goals and fizzled out of the World Cup at the venue of their 1950 triumph.

Round of 16

Late Dutch double melts Mexico

Netherlands 2 Mexico 1 (Fortaleza)

The Netherlands came from behind to beat Mexico with 2 very late goals in the searing heat of Fortaleza.

The first half was dictated by the heat, but 3 minutes after the break Giovani dos Santos chested the ball into his stride and whacked it into the corner of the net from 25 yards out. Ochoa made a point blank save from de Vrij in the 57th minute, diverting his effort onto the post and blocked an angled shot from Robben who had skipped into the box in the 74th minute, but he was finally beaten in the 88th minute when a corner was headed back by Huntelaar into the path of Wesley Sneijder who smashed in a bullet.

With extra time looming, Robben went down in the box and Klaas Jan Huntelaar sent Ochoa the wrong way from the spot with an accurate shot into the bottom left corner.

Round of 16

Ten tired Costa Ricans win shootout

Costa Rica 1 Greece 1 (Recife)
Costa Rica win on penalties

Greece took 10-man Costa Rica to penalties and lost.

Costa Rica scored in the 52nd minute when the ball was laid on to Bryan Ruiz who spun it low into the corner of the net from just outside the box, but in the 66th minute Duarte was dismissed for a second yellow, and as the Costa Ricans began to tire, Greece pushed forward and in stoppage time Gekas turned in the box and struck a low shot that Navas could only parry into the path of Sokratis Papastathopoulos who hit the ball into the ground and over the keeper to give the Greeks a 30 minute lifeline which they wouldn't have needed had Navas not tipped Mitroglou's header acrobatically over the bar with the clock ticking away in stoppage time.

With no goals in extra time and after successful penalties from Borges, Mitroglou, Ruiz, Christodoulopoulos, Gonzalez, Holebas and Campbell, Costa Rican keeper Navas made a splendid save from Gekas leaving Umana to dispatch his penalty high into the corner of the net and take Costa Rica through.

Round of 16

France see off Nigeria

France 2 Nigeria 0 (Brasilia)

Two late goals ended Nigeria's participation in the World Cup.

    Enyeama saved from a Pogba volley in the 22nd minute and in the 77th minute a long corner-kick reached Benzema whose angled effort was cleared as far as Cabaye who hit the underside of the bar from outside the box on the right, but 2 minutes later, after Enyeama had turned Benzema's header over the bar, the Nigerian keeper flapped the resulting corner onto the head of Progba who nodded in for France.

    In the 84th minute Griezmann got into the box from the left and let fly only to see his effort beaten away by the keeper, but the match was put to bed in stoppage time when a low cross into the 6-yard box from a short corner went in off Yobo for an own goal.

Round of 16

Heroic Algeria take Germans to the wire

Germany 0 Algeria 0 (Porto Alegre) **2-1 a.e.t.**

Germany needed extra time to overcome the gutsy Algerians.

Mbohli made a double save in the 40th minute keeping out a shot from Kroos and the follow up from Götze and in the 55th minute dived to get his fingertips to a well-struck shot from Lahm. The Algerian keeper also made a point-blank save from a Müller header 10 minutes from time, but his opposite number, Neuer, had to rush out of his area on many occasions during the match to beat the attacking Algerians to the ball.

Two minutes into extra time Müller delivered the ball into the 6-yard box for Andre Schürrle to heel-flick past the keeper and in the last minute of extra time when Schürrle's effort was cleared off the line Mesut Özil smashed home the rebound, but Algeria had the last word when Feghouli crossed the ball onto the foot of Djabou who slammed in a farewell goal in stoppage time.

Round of 16

Argentina through at the death

Argentina 0 Switzerland 0 (Sao Paulo) **1-0 a.e.t.**

Switzerland came close to taking Argentina to a penalty shootout but fell at the last hurdle.

Drmic was clear on goal for Switzerland in the 39th minute but failed to lob the keeper and in the 62nd minute Benadlio tipped Higuain's header over the bar.

The Swiss keeper got down well to keep out a shot from Messi in the 78th minute and in the 18th minute of extra time he dived to palm away a shot from di Maria, but with 2 minutes left, Messi began a run and passed the ball to di Maria who swiped home into the far corner.

Switzerland almost forced penalties in stoppage time when Dzemaili's header came of the base of the post and out off his knee.

Round of 16

Belgium knock out stubborn Americans

Belgium 0 USA 0 (Salvador) **2-1 a.e.t.**

Tim Howard made a record number of saves to take Belgium to extra time.

The Belgians showed intent from the start when Origi got into the box after less than a minute but saw his effort blocked by the leg of Howard. The American custodian dealt with everything that was thrown at him until 3 minutes into extra time when substitute Lukaku ran into the box from the right and his ball fell to Kevin de Bruyne who turned past his marker and fired in from the edge of the 6-yard box.

Just before the break de Bruyne laid the ball on to Lukaku in the box who dispatched it into the net, but 2 minutes after the changeover Bradley floated the ball into the box over the head of Julian Green who toe-poked his volley past Courtois to give America hope. The Americans came close with 6 minutes remaining when a cleverly taken free kick reached Dempsey but Courtois foiled his effort to make sure of a Belgian quarter-final place against Argentina.

Quarter final

Germany head to semi

Germany 1 France 0 (Rio de Janeiro)

A 1-0 victory over France gave Germany a place in the semi-finals.

The only goal of the match came in the 12th minute when a free kick from the left was crossed into the box for Mats Hummels to side-head in off the bar. In the 34th minute Neuer parried Valbuena's angled volley, but Benzema's close-range follow up was foiled by Hummels.

In the second half, as the French half-heartedly pushed forward, the Germans threatened on the break and in the 82nd minute Özil got into the box and pulled the ball back to Schürrle via a Müller air shot, but his effort was blocked by the legs of Lloris. Deep into stoppage time Benzema forced his way into the box after a quick one-two, but his angled shot was swatted away together with any hope France may have had of rescuing the game.

Friday July 4th

Quarter final

Brazil end Colombian run

Brazil 2 Colombia 1 (Fortaleza)

Hosts Brazil moved on to the semi-final stage with a 2-1 win over Colombia but will be without star player Neymar who was carried off injured and captain Thiago Silva who will be suspended after picking up another booking.

It was Silva who opened the scoring when he turned the ball in at the far post from a corner kick after only 7 minutes.

The early goal was the difference between the 2 teams until the 69th minute when David Luis unleashed a superb free kick from 35 yards to double Brazil's lead, but in the 78th minute Cesar brought Bacca down in the box and was sent the wrong way by James Rodriguez who bowed out of the competition with 6 goals to his name.

Quarter final

Argentina sroll along to semi

Argentina 1 Belgium 0 (Brasilia)

Gonzalo Higuain scored for Argentina to knock out pre-tournament dark horses Belgium.

The only goal of the match came in the 8th minute when a pass was deflected to Higuain who swiped an instinctive volley from just inside the box past the rooted Courtois.

In the 55th minute Higuain picked the ball up in his own half, ran through the Belgian defence into the box and bounced the ball off the bar, and with Belgium unable to find a goal to force extra time Messi broke through in stoppage time but couldn't get past Courtois.

Saturday July 5th

Quarter final

Krul end for brave Costa Rica

Netherlands 0 Costa Rica 0 (Salvador)
Netherlands win on penalties

Tim Krul came off the bench to save 2 penalties in a shootout and end Costa Rica's fairy tale run.

Having already blocked several Dutch efforts, Navas dived brilliantly to his right in the 39th minute to keep out a 35-yard free kick from Sneijder who in the 82nd minute curled a free kick from the left corner of the box onto the near post. Two minutes later, after a poor clearance, Navas blocked an angled shot from van Persie who also failed to connect in front of goal in the 89th minute and as the Dutch piled on the pressure to avoid extra time Blind's delivery into the danger zone eluded everyone before reaching van Persie whose shot was frantically cleared off the line and onto the bar by Tejeda in stoppage time.

In the 3rd minute of extra time Navas dived to push away a header form Vlaar, but with 3 minutes remaining it was Cillessen who saved the day with a vital block when Ureña ran at the Dutch defence and fired from inside the box. A minute from time Sneijder struck the crossbar from the edge of the area and just before the final whistle Krul replaced Cillessen in goal to steal the limelight from man-of-the-match Navas by saving 2 penalties from Ruiz and Umana and taking the Netherlands into the last four.

Tuesday July 8th

Semi final

Brazil torn to pieces

Brazil 1 Germany 7 (Belo Horizonte)

Germany are in seventh heaven after annihilating hosts Brazil 7-1 to reach the final of the World Cup.

Thomas Müller lost his marker with ease from a corner kick in the 11th minute to side-volley the ball in, and in the 23rd minute Müller left the ball to Miroslav Klose who sidefooted it past Cesar on his second attempt, breaking the all-time World Cup scoring record. A minute later a low cross from the right reached Toni Kroos who fired in a left-footer from 18 yards out and almost straight from the restart Brazil were caught in possession and Kroos sent Khedira through who teed the ball back for him to slot in the fourth.

Germany made it 5 in the 29th minute when, in similar fashion to their fourth goal, Özil teed up Sami Khedira to pick his spot. After the break the shell-shocked Brazilians briefly came out of their shell forcing Neuer into action, blocking a shot from Oscar in the 52nd minute and making a brilliant double save from Paulinho a minute later, but in the 61st minute Cesar dived to push Müller's shot over the bar and 8 minutes later he was beaten for the sixth time when Andre Schürrle knocked in Lahm's pass from just outside the 6-yard box.

In the 79th minute, after a throw-in from the left and a beautiful reverse pass from Müller, Khedira smashed the ball in off the bar from a tight angle to make it 7 and in the 90th minute Özil came inches from making it 8 when he was through on goal but rolled the ball wide of the post. Brazil Immediately broke through with Oscar getting into the box and cutting inside to fire past Neuer and ruin the jubilant Germans' clean sheet.

Semi final

Argentina win final spot

Argentina 0 Netherlands 0 (Sao Paulo)
Argentina win on penalties

Sergio Romero made 2 saves in a penalty shootout against the Netherlands to send Argentina through to the final of the World Cup.

In an uneventful match Robben was tackled by Mascherano in the box as he was about to pull the trigger in stoppage time and 5 minutes from the end of extra time Palacio failed to lob the Dutch keeper with a weak header.

In the penalty shootout Romero saved Vlaaar's weak penalty with ease, Messi sent Cillessen the wrong way, Robben fired into the bottom corner away from the keeper, Garay smashed in his shot while Romero saved superbly from Sneijder before Aguero slipped the ball under the diving Dutch keeper. Kuyt sent the keeper the wrong way to keep the Dutch alive, but needing to save, Cillessen could only push Maxi Rodriguez's thumping shot in off the bar to spark Argentinian celebrations.

Saturday July 12th

Third place

Dutch bury Brazil for bronze

Brazil 0 Netherlands 3 (Brasilia)

Hosts Brazil lost their second match in a row as the Netherlands claimed third place in the 2014 World Cup.

Thiago Silva escaped with a yellow card after tugging back Robben, who was through on goal in the 2nd minute, and though the offence seemed to have taken place a fraction outside the box, a penalty was awarded which Robin van Persie dispatched into the top corner.

In the 16th minute David Luis headed an innocuous ball into the path of Daley Blind who unchallenged picked the top corner to double the Dutch lead.

In stoppage time Janmaat ran onto a pass from Robben on the right and spun the ball back from the byline for GeorginioWijnaldum to put past Cesar at the near post and condemn Brazil to another embarrassing defeat.

The final

Germany win World Cup in Brazil

Germany 0 Argentina 0 (Rio de Janeiro) **1-0 a.e.t.**

Mario Götze scored in extra time as Germany beat Argentina 1-0 at the Maracana to win the 2014 World Cup.

A misplaced header from Kroos sent Higuain clear on goal in the 21st minute but he scuffed his shot and in stoppage time Höwedes thumped his close-range header from a corner against the Argentine post.

Messi, who had threatened Germany with several runs in the first half, came close 2 minutes after the break when his shot from inside the box narrowly missed the far post.

In the first minute of extra time Schürrle's angled shot from the edge of the 6-yard box was beaten away by Romero and 6 minutes later at the other end Palacio lifted the ball over Neuer but wide of the post. The winning goal came in the 23rd minute of extra time when Schürrle crossed the ball from the left onto the chest of Götze who slid his volley past Romero into the far corner making Germany the first European side to win the World Cup outside Europe.

www.ingramcontent.com/pod-product-compliance
Lightning Source LLC
Chambersburg PA
CBHW060039040426
42331CB00032B/1734